Words for the Heart

From over 40 years of Marriage

Poetry by

Ed Roberts

ISBN 978-1979742337
Published November 2017

All rights reserved.
No part of this publication may be reproduced, stored in a
retrieval system, or transmitted in any form or by any means,
electronic, mechanical, recording or otherwise, without the prior written
permission of Ed Roberts
Manufactured in the United States of America.

Table of Contents ---

I Can't Write the Words	4
I Know, You've Heard It All Before	6
Let's Do Nothing Tonight	8
Three Simple Words	10
Nothing But Each Other	11
A Night in the Hallway	13
Come with Me	15
I Found a Few Words	17
I Tried Hard Not To Love You	18
How Can I Say	20
Love, Hit and Miss	21
A Special Love	22
Untitled	23
Remember	24
Heart Strong	25
I Tried to Paint a Picture	27
I Thought I Knew How Much	28
I May Never Be	30
We All Need Someone	31
Someone at the End of the Day	33
Used Bride	34
Powerless	35
Passion	36
Not in so many words	38
Pure Love	40
He Takes Her a Flower	43
The First 50 Years	45
Fifty Years	47
She Loved Him Once	49
I Can Still Remember My First Love	52
I Thought I Knew	54
Every Time	56
A Special Valentine	58
One Last Dance	60
Love of a Simple Man	61
Forever	63
Last Kiss Before You Leave	64
Letha	65

I Can't Write the Words

I can't write the words
To tell you how I feel
How much that my heart hurts
Whenever you're not here
How hard it is I pray
Just to have another day
To be here by your side
But no matter how hard I try
I can't write the words

Sittin here
I can see everything I have
And you know
It makes me very glad
That you are here
You see
It doesn't matter much to me
A house or a car
It just matters where you are
That's where I wanna be
I gotta be
You see
My life was just an empty page
Then you came along
You wrote every song
Made my heart play along
With yours
It's sad
That I keep sitting here
Trying to write a simple song
Just to let you know that you belong
Here by my side
But no matter how hard I try
I just can't write the words

I can't write the words
To tell you how I feel
How much that my heart hurts
Whenever you're not here
How hard it is I pray
Just to have another day
To be here by your side
But no matter how hard I try
I can't write the words

No
You make the music
But I just can't write
The words

Ed Roberts 2/22/01

I Know, You've Heard It All Before

If I were to tell you
That I love you
It wouldn't impress you much
I know
I can't tell you
How many times
That I've told you this before

If I were to tell you
That I build my life around you
I know
It wouldn't mean a lot
Because again
These are words
That you have already heard

If I were to say
That I can't picture
Where I would be
If I hadn't met you
I doubt you would even stop
To think for a moment
Because we met so long ago

If I stopped for just a second
Just like I am doing now
To try and tell you
All of these things
Hopefully you will stop to listen
And realize
That I never say any of these things
Without meaning
And take them to heart
Even though
I know
You've heard it all before

Ed Roberts 9/04/01

Let's Do Nothing Tonight

Let's do nothing tonight
No TV
No movies
Not a dinner out somewhere
Let's go no place
Just stay at home
And do nothing

We could talk about what we did today
Now
That would be something new
We could order in some pizza
Or heat the leftovers from the fridge
You know
I did read a good book the other day
I could tell you about it
If you want
Or not

We could talk about tomorrow
Or maybe what to do this weekend
Or
We could just talk
Now
Wouldn't that be a change
Me wanting to talk
But I am good at listening as well
Who knows
It could be fun

We've got some cards
That have been sitting in the drawer for years now
Or the scrabble game
I think it's still stashed away
Under the bed

We used to enjoy playing games with each other
I bet we still remember how
If not
We can make up our own rules
That sounds like fun
Doesn't it

And tomorrow
When those nosey people at work
Ask you what you did last night
You can look them square in the face
And guess what
You don't even have to make anything up
Just tell them
We did nothing last night
Only they don't have to know
Just how fun doing nothing can really be

Let's do nothing tonight

Ed Roberts 3/26/02

Three Simple Words

The whisper of a moment
Stolen
From the madness of the day
So simple
Yet never unnoticed
As you are heading out the door
The way they seem to flow
Almost effortlessly
From your mouth
But not without feeling
I could never imagine them
Any other way
Three simple words
On which
I can base my whole day
And
My whole life

I LOVE YOU

Ed Roberts 1/29/01

Nothing But Each Other

To many
We had nothing

No video games
No X Boxes
No computers
We had no cell phones
No VCR's
DVD players
There wasn't
This latest gadget or that
Left lying on the floor
Or shoved into the closet somewhere

No
It was nothing like that at all

We had only one television
One phone
And an old car
That by today's standards
Was more the size of a bus
We had second-hand furniture
Last year's clothes
Or even the year's before that
We each had two pairs of shoes
One for school
And one for church
Nothing more
But nothing less

Yes
To many we had nothing
Yet we had the one thing
That money couldn't buy
No manufacturer could ever build
And it seemed that everyone was trying to find

We had love
We had joy
And most of all
We simply had each other
Even in today's world
Could you ever ask for anything more

Ed Roberts 12/19/04

Happiness doesn't come in a box
It can't be bought on E-Bay
Ordered on Amazon
Or found on the shelf at Wal-Mart

It can only start in one's heart
And is most often found
Where nothing else exists
But a smile
A laugh
And most important of course
Where there is love

A Night in the Hallway

The Oklahoma weather raged all around us
We watched the television
Until the power went out
Yep
This one was building every minute
We stopped for a moment
Each holding a flashlight
Stood there just looking at each other
Said the same thing at the same time
This one was going to be
CLOSE

My wife found the battery-powered radio
I started taking the cushions off the sofas
And laid them along the walls of the hallway
It was too late to try and leave
We were going to have to try and ride this one out
At home

The tornado was about 10 miles away
When we went into the hallway
We lay there
Side-by-side on the floor
Pulled a bag of blankets on top of us
And waited
It didn't take long

We could hear the hail and rain
As it beat against the rooftop
The wind as it slammed into the house
Then
For just a moment
It stopped
The quiet was frightening
Everything froze
Then suddenly the rage returned
With new fury

They had lost site of the funnel
We heard it pass over
Just above the rooftop
A cold burst of air crept
 From under all the doors
At once
Damn
I thought
There go the windows

Moments later it was over
We just lay there
I could feel her every breath
I thought to myself
God, how I love this woman

Here we had been
All of nature's fury had raged down around us
The "Finger of God"
Had just spared us from being eaten by the storm
And all the time that I laid there in the hallway
The one thing that I remember the most
Was how much I loved the smell of her cologne

Ed Roberts 5/22/03

Come with Me

Come with me
Let's sit on the shore

Of a babbling brook
Put our problems on a single leaf
And follow it downstream
Until it disappears from sight
Let's catch a moonbeam
Ride it
As it dances across the meadows
Of an oh so still night
Let's swim with the dolphins
Walk with the elephants
Get caught up
In the power of a spring storm
Stop and not smell the roses
Let's inhale them
Fill our lungs with their pollen
And then enjoy
One big sneeze
Let's do all these things
Right now
Or
We can just get back to work
Or sit back
And watch the TV
But wait

There's a fire in the fireplace
And a good book on the shelf
Maybe we could just talk
Or listen to the song of the night outside
Nature has been waiting
Way too long
Just outside the door

Come with me

Let's go

Ed Roberts 3/22/01

I Found a Few Words

I found a word today
It is hope
I found it behind the eyes of my son
As he stood in the doorway and said
Don't worry about me Dad
I really do have a plan for the rest of my life

I found a new word today
It is peace
I found it behind the eyes of my Grandmother
As she leaned forward in her recliner
Just to give me a hug
When I came over to visit

I found a new word today
It is love
I found it in the smile my wife gave me
As she left on her way to work
After I told her that I hoped to write something today

I found a new word today
It is magic
I found it lying here in the shadows
Left by the morning sun
As it shines across the keyboard
As my fingers try ever so hard
To capture these few words
Whispered by my soul

A life surrounded by
Hope, peace, love, and magic
Can anyone ever ask
For anything more

Ed Roberts 2/25/04

I Tried Hard Not To Love You

I tried hard
Not to love you

You hit me like a tsunami
Flooded every crevice
Filled my body
My heart
My soul
I ran
From nothing but fear
I had never been touched so close
So deeply
Like the tide
You pulled me back
For deep down I knew
Where I wanted to spend my nights

I tried hard
Not to love you

You fell upon me
Like an avalanche
Covered my days
My nights
Every moment
With thoughts of you
I ran for no reason
Other than pride
How could you make me appear
 So weak
But it was your warmth
That brought me back
For I knew I could not survive
In the cold
Alone

I tried hard
Not to love you

You blinded me like the sun
All others disappeared
Around you
I ran simply out of worry
Afraid I would become addicted
To something as simple as your smile
But away from you
There was merely darkness
I came back
Because I needed your light
Just to live

Yes
I tried hard
Not to love you

I finally realized
I do
And I know I always will

Ed Roberts 10/19/04

How Can I Say

How can I say
What has already been said before
Without leaving out the meaning
Which is so much harder to ignore
Can one gaze at all the stars
In the middle of the night
Or listen to a nightingale
Once it has taken flight
Then how then can I tell you
Of these feelings that I possess
Can the words ever be spoken
That can rival a gentle caress
As the deserts have sand
And all the spring mornings have dew
Neither can compare
To the love that I have for you

So these words to you I've written
On paper and by hand
But their importance goes much deeper
Than paper can ever hope to span
Just to say " I Love You " seems so simple
But at least I gave it a try
And forever I'll keep trying
Even long after the day that I die

Ed Roberts (date unknown)

Love, Hit and Miss

I brought you flowers
You would have preferred kisses
I bought you diamonds
You would have preferred
The hours the overtime took away instead
I gave you an anniversary card
You would have preferred a simple
I Love You

All these things
I worked so hard to give you
And yet
I missed the most simple
I never stopped to ask

I'll never try and give you the world again
I hope that you'll be happy
With just
My time
My attention
And most of all
My heart

I promise
I'll love you forever

Ed Roberts 7/09/03

Here are two poems I found tucked away in a notebook
I had to have written these while Letha and I were still dating

A Special Love

A special place
A special time
A special kiss
A special rhyme
A special smile
That shines all day
A special love
In every way
A special love
With two that care
A special love
In which they share
A special day
That never ends
A special coin
That's never spent
A special way
In which they care
A special dream
Which together they share
A special love
For you and me
A special vision
We both can see
A special day
That's never through
A special pair
That's me and you
A special way
In which we live
A special way
In which we give
A special love

Ed Roberts (date unknown)

Untitled

When I was just a babe
Reaching out in life for love
Your tender hand I found
It's always you I'm thinking of
As I grew in a world of hurt
A cushion eased the pain
And as sorrow poured upon me
Your umbrella stopped the rain
In my darkest deepest hour
When blackness closed my mind
You were there a lamp that was burning
Shining brightly with love and peace so kind
When my world fell down upon me
And shattered me like glass
You were there with glue and stickle
To gather up the mass
Oh if I were to last forever
And stayed past all is through
I'd give to God my entire lifetime
Just to pass today with you

Ed Roberts (date unknown)

I wrote this one for my son Adam

Remember

She doesn't always know or care
What's "cool" to you
She doesn't have to like everything you do

She won't always tell you what she wants you to do
Sometimes she'll make you ask
But there always is something she has in mind

She always will want to know where you are
Even when you are just hanging out

Give her flowers
Even when it's not her birthday or your anniversary
Or you have done something wrong

Never forget her birthday or YOUR anniversary

Nothing ever makes her butt look big
Even if it does

Learn to disagree on some things
But never expect her to tell you when you were right

And never forget the 5 most important words

I LOVE YOU

And

YES DEAR

Ed Roberts (date unknown)

Back to more written for Letha

Heart Strong

I know I'm the one
Who is supposed to be
Strong

I kill the spiders
And any other
Creepy-crawly
That wonders into the house

If something
Needs to be moved
I move it

If something
Needs to be lifted it
I lift it

If someone were
To break into the house
They would have to go through me
To get to you
And they wouldn't
Not as long
As I am alive

I can take a beating
I can take the pain

I literally
And figuratively
Can take almost anything
Life has
Or can
Throw my direction

Yes
I am the one
Who is supposed to be strong

I just wanted to take a moment
A rest bit from the chaos
We call "normal'
And remind you
My darling

I am only this strong
Because you give me
The love
And the passion
To be this way

I am
What I am
Because of you

With love

Ed Roberts 5/15/17

I Tried to Paint a Picture

I tried to paint a picture
Of what my life would be like

Without you

The canvass is still blank
You are my inspiration
The words
And the music
To my every song

26 years have come and gone
Since the day I made you my wife

And of all the things that I sometimes
Tend to forget
This is one
I will always remember
Because you became
Oh so much more

You became my very life

Ed Roberts 10/17/02

Sometimes I do write for others when it comes to love.
This next poem was for a friend
I think it defines love in a way few can imagine

I Thought I Knew How Much

I thought I knew
How much she loved me

We were married for forty years
We had two children together
Fine young men
They are now

Yes
I thought I knew
How much she loved me

And even when the cancer came
Attacked her body in ways you can not imagine
She still held my hand
You'd have thought I was the one who was dying
She was there for me
Until her time here was done

Yes
I thought I knew
How much she loved me

It was just yesterday
I found it there
Hidden away in the back of her closet
A small box
Filled with a bundle of letters
All wrapped with a single red ribbon

I read through each of these
Letters with words filled with such emotion
They spoke of nights of wonder
Stolen moments of pleasure
And dreams of a lifetime of happiness

Yes
I thought I knew
How much she loved me

Each letter I read
Even when the tears blocked my eyes
Even when my body shook
I read each and every letter
And then
And only then
Did I truly understand

Here she had kept this box of letters
Precious memories
Words filled with such passion
And not a single one of these
Were mine

Now
I understand just how much she loved me
Because she had him
And all of these wonderful letters
Yet, married me instead

God
I miss her so much

Ed Roberts 3/8/08

Again more for Letha

I May Never Be

I may never be a millionaire
I know I'll never make anywhere near that much
I'll never be a super star
I'm not a man with that much luck
I'll never be a hero
Or have my face shown on TV
I'll never be a lot of things
But darling
I will always be
Me

Yes
I'm the one
That said he would love until the end of time
And I would give you anything
There's nothing that I will keep
As mine
I'll be there for good times
And you know
That I'll also be here for the bad

When your world would come down
Upon you
And your troubles seem to crush you to the floor
I'll be right there
To support you
And I promise
Each day
I will love you
Even More

Ed Roberts 2/08/02

We All Need Someone

We all need someone
Someone that we can call
When we really have nothing to say
Someone we can share our triumphs with
Even if they are "little" ones
Someone we share our defeats with
Even if the rest of the world doesn't seem to give a damn

We all need someone
Someone we can call out to
When the shadows are closing in
When we are left stranded
Alone sitting on the highway of life
We all need someone
Someone there that we know will pick up

We all need someone
Someone who would drive through a rainstorm
Just to bring us an umbrella
Or just offer a strong shoulder to cry on
Or a hand to hold
When everything seems to be slipping away

We all need someone
Someone that will listen
And not be afraid to speak up
Even though they know
We probably won't listen to a thing they have to say

We all need someone
Someone to share our laughs
Dry our tears
Someone who in the end
Really needs us there as well

As for me
I was very lucky to find that someone
Luckier still
I married her
And she doesn't seem to mind
There are so many other "someones"
Out there as well.

Ed Roberts 11/18/06

These next two poems I wrote for my mother and her second husband A.C.
It is never too late to find love

Someone at the End of the Day

An empty house
So many empty rooms
Empty days
Made up of so many empty hours
Some may look at it this way
Growing old

But a house has doors that can be opened
Empty rooms can easily become cluttered
And empty days or hours
Can be filled with precious moments

Sometimes whether people think it is right
Or wrong
Does not matter
In life
Too soon is often far better
Than too late

At the end of even the shortest of days
We all need someone
That someone special
That will be there just for us
Even if all we need
Is for them to be there
At the end of each day
To be that someone
Willing to turn off the light

Ed Roberts 6/12/07
(For Mom and A.C.)

Used Bride

Bride
As is
High mileage
Definitely not in new condition
No warranty implied
No returns
Given to groom
In same condition as above
With love

Ed Roberts 2/01/08

Inspired by the movie " Bruce Almighty " for Letha

Powerless

On a whim
I can change the course of a mighty river
With but a glance
I can turn off the Sun
And turn it back on again
My breath controls the winds
My tears the rain
Each one of my smiles
Makes a flower bloom
All that you see
All that you know
Is because of me
And yet
Here now I stand before you
Powerless
For I know
I could destroy the Earth
And remake it three times in my own image
But it is the one thing
That you control
That gives you rule over me

Yes
I can make and unmake so many things
Almost everything
But with all my power
There is but one thing beyond my reach
I still can not make you love me
This you will have to learn how to do
On your own

Ed Roberts 6/09/03

Sometimes we simply look at love without thinking seeing this

Passion

Every time our bodies touch
Is it as if
A starving man suddenly awakes
And finds himself
In the midst of a banquet
A drowning man
Finally gets that much anticipated
First gulp of fresh air
Not only do our bodies come together
Our minds melt
And our souls dance
As they slowly fuse
Into one
The passion inside
Roars
Expands until it has tested
Every seam of my fiber
My heart crashes against my chest
Like ocean waves
Against the ever-yielding rocks at the shore
The pressure builds
Until even the ground beneath my feet
Crumbles into dust
Finally
The calm comes
I stand before you
Fulfilled
And emptied at the same time
But always hungry for more

Who would have thought
Even in their greatest fantasy
That a human could withstand
This great amount of pleasure
And all of it
All of this that I have tried
Fought to describe to you
Could be given to one single lucky person
By just
A simple kiss

Ed Roberts 11/10/02

Next, a poem written for a friend to help understand the love of her father

Not in so many words

He said I love you
But not always in so many words

But you could see it there
In the way he smiled
When he brushed your hair
The way he'd stay and watch you
Until you fell asleep
The way he'd pick you up
When you fell
The way
He'd kiss away your boo-boos
And your tears
In the way
He'd worry about you
When you were late
Question you
On where you'd been
Or who you were with
At the time you thought he was prying
Trying to rule over your life
Now it is so much easier to understand
Since you have a child of your own

You could see it
In the way he always put what you wanted
In front of what he desired
And even sometimes of what he needed
To see your smile meant so much
Each laugh for him
Was like a gift from Heaven

They say with age the vision fades
And the mind slips away into memories
But everyday that you grow older
You realize
You come to understand
That everyday you spent with your Father
He always said I love you
Just not always in so many words

Ed Roberts 11/25/04

Sometimes we have to look at others before we can truly understand love. I wrote this for a friend, Barbara

Pure Love

So few people understand the nature
Of pure love

For so many years
Barbara would support her husband Daniel
During the week
She would come home from work
And start cooking supper
More times than not
She would have dinner waiting for him
When he came through the door
She would do the laundry
Clean the dishes
Everything it took
To keep the house clean

So few people understand the nature
Of pure love

On oh so many weekends
Barbara would support her husband Daniel
Together they would drive several miles
Sometimes stay overnight in different small towns
And she would sit in the stands
Often with many strangers
And watched and cheered
As Daniel rode bulls

Bull riding was his passion
Something he had done most of his life
He did have the scars to prove this
And in so many ways
So did she

One Sunday in October
Everything changed
While riding a bull named "Destroyer"
Daniel was thrown just outside the corral gate
Like so many times before
He hit the ground hard
But this time
He landed first on his head
Barbara was there
When they loaded him into the ambulance
She was there waiting
While they worked to save his life
And she was also there
When they told him
He would never walk again
That for the rest of his life
He would only be able to move
His left arm

So few people understand the nature
Of pure love

Some women would have left
Especially during the first few months
The months Daniel said
He wished that he had died that day
She understood he was hurting
She understood that he was angry
She understood him in ways
That he didn't understand himself

In the ten years that followed
Barbara would support her husband Daniel
She was with him
When he learned to eat again
When he learned how to operate his new chair
And also when he learned to drive again
She went with him
When he went to Wal-Mart

To apply for a greeter position
And took off work to drive him there
For his first day of work
She was also there
The day they took him to the hospital
And a few days later
When they turned off the machine
That had breathed for him for his last five days

So few people understand the nature
Of pure love

I am writing these words for you tonight
Because in my life I have met some special people
People who I feel need to have their story told
A story I know they will never write
For themselves

A story of a man who chose to ride bulls
And the story of a woman who stood by his side
And never thought or demanded anything for herself

So few people understand the nature
Of pure love

I wanted to write these words
Because Barbara did

Ed Roberts
12/15/13

I wrote this next poem for one of my neighbors

He Takes Her a Flower

He takes her a flower
Every afternoon
And reads to her
Each night
He knows deep inside
That she'll be leaving soon
But he makes sure
That she never sees him cry
Every night
Before he gets up to leave
He bends over to kiss her cheek
And in a voice loud enough
For only her to hear
He whispers softly in her ear

I'm still here
Though it's hard to see
Deep inside this shell of a man
You know honey
That its still me
I know that you can't walk
And it doesn't matter that you can't talk
You know I'll still love you for all time
Darling every night
I can still hold you tight
And we dance together
In my dreams
Now please try to go to sleep
You know that I'll be right outside
And tomorrow
If I wake
I'll be back here once again

Every night
As he turns to leave
A single tear rolls down her cheek
There's so much that she would love to say
If only her lips still remembered
How to speak
And she knows that she'll be leaving soon
But till then she has to wait
As she slowly drifts off to sleep
He's there waiting once again
He takes her close
Into his arms
And they dance the night away again
And she tells him

I'm still here
Though it's hard to see
Deep inside this shell of a woman
Honey you know
That its still me
I know that I can't walk
God I wish that I could talk
But at least you know
That I'll love you for all time
And in the morning
When I wake
I know you'll be here by my side
And if I don't
I just hope you know
That I'll try to be here for you
Forever for all time

He takes her a flower
Every afternoon

Ed Roberts 8/1/01

I wrote this for a special couple who are friends with my mother

44

The First 50 Years

It was so long ago
And so far away
But sometimes it seems
Like it was just yesterday

We were just strangers
And then so much in love
We built a life from nothing but dreams
Under the sky above
We bought our first house
Bought our first car
We mapped out our future
But we didn't plan far
It was so hard to imagine
Just those first five years
We grew so quickly together
We faced so many different fears

Before we knew it
It had been twenty
Our children came
Then they were gone
We just leaned on each other
God knows how we got along

Thirty years came
And they went so fast
When we hit forty
We weren't sure that it would last

But now here we are
Fifty years and going strong
Who would have even thought
That we'd make it together this long

Tomorrow we'll start
With a love like it just began
And when this life for us is over
We'll meet together in a better place
And start it all over
Once again

Ed Roberts 6/03/02

Dedicated to Billie & Olen Smith on their 50th anniversary
1952 - 2002

And I wrote the next poem for another couple who had met that mile stone, I pray my wife and I will get there

Fifty Years

Fifty years
18,270 days
438,480 hours
Give or take a few
A long time to some
A blink of an eye to others
So many good days
Yes, a few bad ones as well
Some moments filled with such emotion
They seem to last forever
Some pass by
Without even making a sound
Some moments
When you feel so apart
Together but alone
And some
Where it does seem that two bodies
Can actually share the same heart
Fifty years
Filled with good mornings
I missed you
A few I'm sorrys when they are needed
And you can't forget the many yes dears
Just to keep the peace
And of course
There are the I love yous
Those special words
That keep everything held together
There can never be too many of those you know
In this world
There are so many things that come and go with time
And some that pass day by day, year by year
Undaunted by even time itself
To find a love like this is to find
One of life's greatest treasures
Two hearts that beat together as one

As they did fifty years ago
As they do today
And as they will do so
Until the end of time

Ed Roberts 2/19/04

(Dedicated to Willard &Janie Speck 1954-2004)

I wrote this for my friend Mary Sue

She Loved Him Once

She loved him once
At least
The man he used to be

When they first met
They were so young
Their lives were filled with many dreams
Filled so much with each other

First it seemed
There was little room for anything else
Then the children came
The first
Then the second
Their love grew
Even enough to cover the third
For she was their little angel

Yes
She loved him once
The man he used to be

Time
As in most cases
Took its toll

The hours of overtime
The worry being the sole provider brought
Chipped away at him
Slowly at first
Visible
Just below the surface
Still he never complained

He was always their superman
The knight in shining armor
When they needed more he found it
But not always without a price

The gray hair came early
It was at their daughter's wedding
She first noticed the shake in his hands
How long had this been going on
She wondered
How hard he had struggled
To make sure she didn't see
She would never know

It didn't take long
Before it didn't matter how hard he tried

She did love him once
The man he used to be

Now in so many ways
He is his own reflection
Gone is the sharpness
His eyes would always reveal
On a good day
He still remembers her
On a bad
He just sits there
Not even knowing his own name

People wonder
Behind her back
And yes
Even sometimes to her face
Why she still stays

Why she hasn't shipped him away somewhere
Why she still cares for him
Twenty-four-seven
At home

Deep down
They know
She did love him once
The man he used to be

What they can't see
Is that she loves him even more

Today

Ed Roberts 10/25/04

Love is not blind
Sometimes it is just harder to see

I could not do this book without including this special poem, it should be easy to tell why

I Can Still Remember My First Love

I can still remember my first love
Her first touch
We were both so timid
At first
It was so new
For both of us
It is hard to forget
You're first love

Through the good times
And the bad
She was there
I often wonder
How she really felt
I wasn't always easy to be around
But it didn't seem to matter
It is hard to forget your first love

Just when it seemed
We were beginning to do it right
Things changed
Times changed
I changed
There were so many new experiences
So many new people
She was still there but different somehow
I guess I changed more than she did
And I found another
But I still remember my first love

I still see her from time to time
My life seems so busy
Yet she doesn't change
And deep inside
My feelings for her still remain
And I know they always will
I will always remember my first love

Even though there have passed
So many names and faces through my life
So many forgotten
Swept away by time
Her name has always been the easiest to remember
And is one I will never forget
Though she has had many different names
Throughout her life
I will always simply refer to her
By her simple name

Mom

Ed Roberts 5/10/1991

Sometimes we think we might know everything, sometimes we prove ourselves wrong

I Thought I Knew

I thought I knew what power was
Until I looked into a storm
And saw the winds
Rip the very pavement
From the Earth

I thought I knew what love was
Until I watched an older couple
As they sat together
In a park on a bench
Just enjoying being together

I thought I knew what hate was
Until I looked upon
What was left of a building
And could do nothing
But just ask why

I thought I knew what pain was
Until I saw the eyes
Of a fireman
Who held a child's body
In his arms
And could do nothing more than cry

I thought I knew what fear was
Until I closed my eyes one night
And knew for sure
That I may not be able
To ever look upon my family again

I thought I knew what the future was
Until I looked into the eyes
On my new grandson
And saw all the tomorrows
That lay before him
And hoped to share with him
All that I possibly can

I thought I knew what life was
But even I have to admit
There is so much left to learn

Ed Roberts 10/17/01

Yes, even after 41 years this is still true

Every Time

Every time we touch
It takes my breath
My knees grow weak
It's like
I'm scared to death

Is it really safe
To be this much in love
To build my world
Around just one heart
Should I risk this much
With so little left behind

Yet
Every time we kiss
My heart just stops
And melts with yours
This can't be wrong
A love like this
Is just too hard to find
Such a moment in time
Could it last like this
Can a flame this strong
Keep burning on
Forever

Every time you leave
You take away my heart
But you leave yours behind
For me to hold
What more can I ask

What words can I write
To describe a love like ours
Is it not enough
That I simply sit here
And try

Every time

Ed Roberts 2/03/02

A lot of people think love poetry is only for holidays, sometimes it is

A Special Valentine

When we first met
We were strangers

I was the new woman
Just another pretty face

You didn't have to be kind
No, there had been others before
They came
They went
Often leaving you to pick up the pieces
Fixing the broken heart
Of one that you love

Days, weeks, months passed
My life changed
So did his
We grew together
And on one special day
We became one
You were there as well

So many years have passed since that day
And you have been here with us as well
With us
You shared the smiles
And even the tears
The good days
And the bad
Like your son
You became such an important part
Of my life

When we met
Yes, we were strangers
No, you didn't have to be kind
You didn't even need to give me the time of day

I just wanted to take this time
Share with you a few special words
And thank you
Because you not only shared with me
Your own special child
Over these so many years
You have given the one thing that mattered most
You shared with me
Your love

(Written for a friend)

Sometimes it is for a special reason

One Last Dance

Come to me
Even though this may be
My death bed
Let our passion
Ravage us
Let our bodies touch
Once more entwine
Until not a single space exists
Even between our souls
Let me drink of your essence
Take one final deep breath
So that I may hold it
Trapped deep inside my chest
Forever
And
If in the morrow
I am granted
Just another single day
To spend upon this Earth
I shall rejoice in it
Knowing
That for one single moment
I was truly
The happiest being
To ever experience
Her warm embrace

Then
Come the setting of the sun
Let us begin this glorious dance
Once again

Ed Roberts 12/01/02

Sometimes is can be very simple

Love of a Simple Man

I sit here trying
To write a "special" Something just for you
It's harder than it looks

You see
It's just not the dinners
The movies
The flowers when I can
Or even the bedroom
Whenever we can
Sure these are special
But you see
I am a simple man
And to me
It's also the dishes
The laundry
The kids
The vacuuming
The cleaning
The kids
The mowing
The raking
Yeah, I know
I already mentioned the kids
But you see
It's all these things
We try and do together

And I have to admit
That at some
I'm not real good
But we try and do it together
And that's what makes it
So special
Each day I have with you

So I'm writing you this poem
And what I guess
That I am trying to say
Is that I really do love you
And you're special
Each and every day

Time is measured by clocks
And numbers on a page
But love is measured
In forever
And the memories
That we are allowed to save
Until all the clocks
Have lost their memory
And all days with numbers
Are through
Until forever is
Ancient history
My love still grows for
You

Ed Roberts 10-06-1995

I did say

Forever

One word
I whisper
To you
Each night
In the dark
Before I close my eyes
Loud enough
Only for your heart
To hear
Just to let you know
How long
My love for you
Will last

FOREVER

Ed Roberts 1/11/01

Some simple things truly mean a lot

Last Kiss Before You Leave

Yes
We have been married forty years
Have been together
Longer than that
And yes
We have had to have shared
A million kisses
Or more
In that time

I am writing this now
Just to let you know
As if you didn't already
That to me
Each one is special
And the one I get each day
Right before you go out the door
To work each morning
Is the most special one of all
Because
Somehow I have to make it last
Until you come back home to me
Again

Of course the one I get then
Is special
Too

With all my love
To Letha

Ed Roberts 2/14/17

One last poem before I leave you.
I literally had to travel across half the world before I could finally sit down and write this

Letha

Letha is my love
Letha is my life
She is the air that I breathe
The second beat of my heart
Or is she the first

By my side she was there
When they said
That I may never walk again

She was there
When I lost my job
More than once
And even when I lost my career

She was there
When I nearly lost my mind
And more times than I can count
My life as well

Many would have packed their things
And run towards the nearest exit
Especially when a woman
That I worked with
Claimed that I had grabbed her breast
Yes
That would have done it for most
But she stayed there by my side
Even through that
Because Letha knew that they were wrong
Those that believed her
For Letha understands the meaning of the word love
And knows there is no woman alive
That I would risk losing her over

As many would say
I would die for her
My Letha
Without hesitation
But more importantly
I will live for her

Every moment
That I am given upon this Earth
With her
I will gladly share

In my dreams
When I reach into the darkness
To pull another body close to mine
She is the one I am reaching for
And every morning when I awake
She is there
Waiting for me still
She truly is the air that I breathe
The well from which my soul drinks

A day has not passed
That I have not stopped for a moment
To thank God in Heaven
For bringing you into my life
And for making you my wife

I love you
Letha
And will do so
Even after the end of time

You are the second beat of my heart
Or maybe
You were the first

Ed Roberts
Written in Amman 9/7/05

Well here you have it
This was a special gift for my wife
One which she has no idea I have been working on for over a year now

I do hope that you have found some words here that have touched your heart as well

With love
Ed

Previous books written by Ed Roberts

A Poet's Last Stand

I'm Still Standing

Everything Must Have a Beginning, a Middle, and an End

Whispers, Tears, Prayers, and Hope

When Words Escape You, You can Use Mine

The Traveler

From the Pill to the Bottle to You

Sometimes We Wait

Web sites-

www.edrobertspoetry.com

www.poetrypoem.com/apoetslaststand

www.youtube.com/amayhem11

To Lisa

Thank you for all you do for me crazy Thursday Fans. It really took over 40 years to write this book

A Roh[signature]
2-24-18